Prayer After Nine Rainy Days and Other Family Prayers

by Pat Corrick Hinton
illustrated by Karen Gundersheimer

Winston Press

Also by Pat Corrick Hinton:
Prayers for Growing and Other Pains

Copyright © 1978, Pat Corrick Hinton
Library of Congress Card Catalog Number: 77-91626
ISBN 0-86683-626-8 (previously ISBN 0-03-042781-9)
Printed in the United States of America

7   6   5   4   3

Winston Press, Inc.
430 Oak Grove
Minneapolis, MN 55403

To God our Father,
    who gifted me with the ability
    to write this book.
To my husband, Jim, and our children,
    Laura and Mark, who are truly
    coauthors.
And to Joan,
    who turned the key.

Contents

Introduction

Many of us parents want to pray with our families and feel dissatisfied with always using traditional meal and bedtime prayers. But sometimes we feel embarrassingly uncomfortable praying in our own words, even within the intimacy of our family circle. This book, in providing prayers for everyday occasions in ordinary words, will help families who want to pray together make the transition from praying traditional, formal prayers together to praying together in their own words.

Why do we want to pray? Because we feel a basic need to let God into our lives, to tell God we see how great he is, and to ask God to share our ups and downs. However, this impulse to pray does not make prayer happen automatically. Prayer needs to be learned through practice to become a habit. God may always be present, but we live our lives in a big rush. To take time to quiet ourselves and communicate with God demands a choice at first. The momentum of each day's events carries us along beyond thought of stopping, beyond having anything to say if we do stop. For the family that chooses to pray together, this book offers words for all the times when family members want to stop and pray but do not yet have words of their own.

Parents often want their family to pray together because they want their children to learn to pray. Children learn the habit of talking with God much as they learn all other good and bad habits—through our example. We parents take our children here and there for sports events, music and dance lessons, club and church meetings. We urge them to master a variety of skills and often in the busyness forget they need to learn how to pray. Since children learn best by doing, they best learn to pray by praying, by talking with God on an everyday, easy basis. They learn to pray by praying with us.

How do we begin to pray together? By making the effort. We search out a time in each busy day when the family is best able to quiet down and be receptive to God's presence. We as parents may feel uneasy and uncertain about praying together when we begin. Learning how to pray ourselves as we pray with our children can be beautiful. We teach them not only that we value praying together, but also that we value learning new things together. In time, we find that prayer is much more natural to us than our fears and discomfort permitted us to realize. But starting is the hardest part.

In prayer we nurture a love-relationship, both with God and with family members. Families develop closeness in many ways, but gathering together to talk over the day with God and each other almost always deepens this closeness. In each prayer time, family members recognize God in their lives and grow a little in the secure feeling that God is surely present in this special group of people on good days and bad.

How early can children learn to pray? Fortunately, it's never too late to learn, but ideally, never too early. Very little children, under age five, can develop a close relationship with God if we give them the opportunity. Never underestimate the power of preschoolers when they learn who God is and why we talk with him. Their natural state of awareness at this age is one of *wonder*, so we can build on their capacity for amazement. When we tell young children of a loving God who made us and helps us and cares about every single thing we do, we are simply opening up an avenue for their natural expression of wonder and joy.

Through trial and error our family has worked out several patterns for praying together; the purpose of this book is to share them with other families. From the time of our first efforts, when our two children were able to sit securely in high chairs, we found the evening meal the best time for family prayer. This is impossible in many families, but a meal does provide a natural occasion for remembering God's goodness. So does bedtime.

In the early years, we were building an *attitude* toward prayer rather than defining certain words that constitute a particular prayer. For example, our "high chair" prayers were very simple, such as the grace from the Romper Room

TV Show: "God is great, God is good; let us thank him for our food." Then, singing our grace became interesting, and a tune learned in preschool religion classes became a favorite: "Praise him, praise him, all the little children. God is love, God is love." Our children didn't pronounce the words *praise* and *love* correctly and probably didn't understand their meanings very well, but they sang with such gusto we knew they had caught the spirit of what they were saying.

Another success was Sebastian Temple's "Praise Be the Lord, Alleluia." Once we even attempted one of our adult favorites, "I Will Raise Him Up." We explained that it meant we'll go to heaven with Jesus someday. In the middle of the song our four-year-old interrupted, "Will we be able to come back here first? 'Cuz I want to get my clothes and take a bath." In another song, for a long time we heard: "The Spirit is amovin' oh-Oliver, oh-Oliver this land." As we listened to our children, we quickly discovered what made sense to them and what only to us.

When the children were about three and a half or four and could better express themselves, we added to our prayer a thank-you to God for some nice thing that had happened that day. As they grew older and played more with other children, they talked to God about problems they were facing. While thinking over the day, they'd remember something "awful" or say, "Do you know what Jimmy did?" We let them tell about it and then added a few words asking God to help that person. Prayerfully thinking over the day is a good habit for all of us, especially if we try to emphasize the good things. Even on a bad day, *something* good must have happened. When we reflect on the good things our Father gives us, we set a happy tone for the meal, instead of letting it become an exercise in discipline or even a battleground.

Slowly our family prayer time helped our children begin to understand that praying is talking to God who made us, loves us, and cares for us. Prayer grows naturally when we pray often, and it gradually encompasses more and more people, needs, and thanks.

As our children learned to read and write, they also developed some ideas of their own on how we could pray together. At present, with our children at ages eleven and nine, we all take turns leading the prayers. Each of us chooses any plan—even writing our own prayers. My husband will often start with the song "Amazing Grace," followed by his particular thanks for the good things of his day and petitions for the needy. The needy may be someone ill at work or people caught in a disaster mentioned in the day's news. We each try to remember something no one else has thought of. We never have trouble thinking of people who need our prayers. As we recall the needs of others, we learn at the same time not to take our blessings for granted.

Our daughter likes to read from a children's book of psalms or from our own collection of prayers; she follows up with thanks and petitions that evolve from her world of school, friends, and family. She often startles us with prayers for the dying, the sad, the lonely, the cold, someone who hurt her feelings. Our son's favorite is to read a story about Jesus from a children's Bible and to show the picture to the rest of the family (the way adults read to children). He almost always prays for his grandparents and the poor. I enjoy beginning the prayer with the song "Oh, the Lord Is Good to Me," or saying the Our Father as we all hold hands. On good days I try to name specific good things that happened. On bad days I thank God for helping me through the day and pray for others who had a bad day but don't have a loving family to help them.

For our family of four, family prayer usually takes around five well-spent minutes, unless we get off on a discussion of a problem we're praying about. (That discussion can be prayerful, too.) Praying with Scripture sometimes takes a little longer.

These are some general ideas about how we pray together, but they also provide a pattern for the times we pray by ourselves.

On some days, for a variety of reasons, it's difficult to pray together. On such days the feelings we bring to a gathering are so strong—in either a positive or a negative way— that we need prayers that come from outside ourselves. The prayers in this book were inspired by those days when it was difficult to pray, *especially* together. The book gives a variety of ideas for praying, for filling in some of those blank spaces of the mind and heart. Included are examples of how to use these prayers or Scripture or simply your own creativeness. Blank pages are provided for the original prayers that will spring from your particular family or circumstances. (You'll be glad later if you write down author and date for every original prayer.)

Even though the book is primarily aimed at helping families with young children, it is not just for children or for two-parent families. The prayers here are for any kind of family at any time of day. Every family (or individual) will have to discover their own best quiet time, and then perhaps these prayers will be stepping-stones toward a more enriching prayer life, whether it be at meals, bedtime, or any other time. Happy praying!

Suggestions for Successful Family Prayer

- Timing is important. Choose a time when family members, especially children, are most receptive.
- Keep prayers short.
- Keep them positive.
- Keep them meaningful.
- Remember that none of us has to be a theologian to be able to talk with God and about him.
- Change the format as often as necessary to keep out of ruts. Variety is also the spice of prayer and the key to attention-holding (this applies to all ages!).
- Take turns leading. As children get older they can plan this for themselves. They love picking out a method of prayer that everyone else will use.

- Light a candle during prayer time, especially in winter.
- Use songs from church or school, something from the children's experience. We discovered that singing at mealtime, even singing a part of a hymn or song learned in church, increases attention and participation at Mass.
- Hold hands often. On "bad" days, when someone is out of sorts, pass "love" around: have one person squeeze the next person's hand and that person squeeze the next one's. Little ones especially love this.
- Encourage children to create their own prayers. One of the most valuable things we can do is to make a child feel that his or her opinion and ideas are great enough to be shared with the whole family. It does wonders for the child's self-image. Listening carefully to their choices of prayers and intentions can reveal insights about the children and lead to valuable conversations.

Sample Plans for Family Prayer

Using this book for family prayer

plan **1**
- The day's leader selects a prayer from this book appropriate to the day.
- This same person reads the prayer for the family at mealtime, bedtime, or your chosen prayer time.

plan **2**
- The day's leader chooses a prayer for the day from this book.
- A family member lights a candle to mark the beginning of family prayer time.
- The leader reads the prayer for the family.

plan 3

- The day's leader selects a prayer and chooses a song to sing at prayer time.
- A family member lights a candle.
- The family sings the song.
- The leader reads the selected prayer.

plan 4

- The day's leader selects a prayer and chooses a song.
- A family member lights a candle.
- The family sings the song.
- The leader reads the selected prayer.
- The family takes a few minutes to think about the prayer and the events of the day.
- Family members pray in their own words about events and people in their day that they want to thank God for or ask God's help for. These prayers might be similar to the following:

Leader: Thank you, God, for my day at school, especially for playing basketball in gym, and for the present Grandma bought. I would like to pray for our sick cousin Dan and for the poor, and that my friends will be nicer to each other.

All: Amen.

Dad: Thank you for helping me through all my paper work and for my friend who helped me with a problem. I'd like to pray for the people who died in the earthquake and their families and for our President and all his helpers.

All: Amen.

Child: Thank you, God, for helping my teacher get well and for Grandma's visit. I'm praying for my friend Joy and for all the sick people and old people in homes and for people who are dying.

All: Amen.

Mom: Thank you, God, for all the good ideas you gave
        me in my writing today and for helping me to
        finally get that cupboard painted. Please help
        those who are lonely and hungry tonight. Help
        us find a way to share what we have.

Using prayers from Scripture for family prayer

Families can use prayers from Scripture for their prayer time
in the same ways they use the prayers in this book. The
following list names some appropriate scriptural prayers and
their biblical references.

o   The Psalms (Choose Psalms appropriate to the children's
    understanding.)
o   Solomon's Prayer—Wisdom 9:1-18 (Select five or six
    appropriate verses.)
o   The Words of God in Nature—Sirach 42:15-25 (Select five
    or six appropriate verses.)
o   Song of Thanksgiving—Isaiah 12:1-5
o   Daniel's Prayer—Daniel 2:20-22

o   The Beatitudes—Matthew 5:3-12
o   The Lord's Prayer—Matthew 6:9-13
o   Jesus' Prayer to His Father—Matthew 11:25-30
o   Mary's Canticle (The Magnificat)—Luke 1:46-55
o   Jesus' Hymn of Praise—Luke 10:21
o   Prayer of Praise—Ephesians 1:3-6
o   Knowing God—Ephesians 1:17-23
o   Prayer for Humility—Philippians 2:6-11
o   Prayer of Thanksgiving—1 Peter 1:3-5
o   We Are Children of God—1 John 3:1-2
o   God's Love and Ours—1 John 4:7-11

Using stories from Scripture for family prayer

Families can use scriptural stories for their prayer time in the
same ways they use prayers from this book or prayers from
Scripture. Children may need help in selecting stories. The

following list supplies the names and biblical references for stories appropriate to children's understanding. (Children will understand Scripture stories better if they read them from a Bible translated especially for children.)

o   Jesus Calls the First Apostles—Matthew 4:18-22
o   Jesus Teaches Us to Pray—Matthew 6:9-13
o   Jesus Chooses Matthew—Matthew 9:9-13
o   Jesus Blesses the Children—Matthew 19:13-15
o   Parable of the Silver Pieces—Matthew 25:14-30
o   Jesus Tells Us How We Should Treat One Another—Matthew 25:34-40
o   Peter Denies Jesus Three Times—Matthew 26:69-75

o   The Christmas Story—Luke 2:1-18
o   Jesus Brings People Together—Luke 4:16-19
o   Jesus Makes Friends—Luke 5:1-11
o   The Good Samaritan—Luke 10:29-36
o   The Prodigal Son—Luke 15:11-32
o   The Last Supper—Luke 22:14-20
o   Jesus' Passion and Resurrection—Luke 22:47-71; 23; 24: 1-9
o   Jesus Appears on the Road to Emmaus—Luke 24:13-35

o   Jesus Washes His Disciples' Feet—John 13:1-17
o   Jesus Tells Us About the Father—John 14:1-21

o   Peter Proclaims the Resurrection—Acts 5:25-39
o   Cornelius Wants to Be a Christian—Acts 10
o   Paul Becomes a Christian—Acts 22:3-16

During family prayer time, the family can use any parts of the plan outlined below.
•   The leader chooses a scriptural story and a song.
•   A family member lights a candle.
•   The family sings the song.
•   The leader reads the selected story.
•   All family members take a few minutes of quiet time to reflect on the story.

- The family discusses the story.

  For example, if the story from Scripture were "The Good Samaritan," parents or older children might initiate a discussion similar to the following:

Mom:	It seems like Jesus is saying we should help people when they need us.
Child 1:	If they ask us, we sure should help.
Dad:	What if they don't ask for help, but we know they need it?
Child 2:	We should help anyway.
Dad:	Can anybody think of a time when you stopped what you were doing to help someone?
Child 1:	I remember picking up Grandpa's wallet when we were playing pool.
Child 2:	I helped Mary go in to the nurse when she fell on the playground.
Dad:	I remember taking a man home from work who lived in a different direction from our house.
Mom:	What about the first two people in the story? They went right on past the hurt man. Sometimes we do that, don't we? We might know somebody needs us, but we're too interested in what we're doing so we pass right by. Let's ask Jesus to help us not to pass by anyone who needs us even if it means we have to stop what we're doing.

- All family members pray silently or the leader reads an appropriate prayer from this book. For example, after discussing "The Good Samaritan," the leader could read "Prayer for Someone I Could Have Helped and Didn't" on page 73 of this book.

Sometimes a discussion of a Bible story will go on through the meal if the family prayer time is at mealtime. Once a week our family reads the Gospel for the coming Sunday and discusses it during our prayer time. When we hear the Gospel at Mass, we all listen with more attention and understanding.

Prayer without a set pattern

Family prayer need not always include a prayer from this book or a prayer or story from Scripture. Occasionally, one person can begin by using his or her own words to say whatever is in his or her mind and heart—praise, thanks, petition, a problem bothering one family member that the whole family can discuss and pray about. Sometimes, only one member of the family wants to pray this way; sometimes, everyone has something to share. Children usually feel comfortable with this kind of spontaneous prayer when the atmosphere invites but does not demand participation.

Prayers for Every Day

Prayer on a Good Day

Loving Father,
so many good things
happened today
it's hard to remember
them all.

Thank you for sharing
all these gifts with us.

We pray
for those who had
a bad day today.

For those who didn't have
enough to eat.

For those who were in pain.

For those who were fighting others.

For those who had
no one to love them.

Help them to have a loving day
tomorrow.

We ask this in the name of Jesus.
Amen.

Prayer on a Day When I Felt Love

Fill in examples from your own day.

God our Father,
you shared your love with me
in many ways
today.

Your love was
in Dad's hug
before he went to work.

Your love was
in the special treat
Mom put in my lunch.

Your love was
in my (sister, brother, friend)
helping me with _____.

Your love was
in my pet _____
snuggling close to me.

Your love was in _____.

Your love is all around me.
Thank you, Father.

Prayer on an Ordinary Day
Fill in examples from your own day.

Loving Father,
this was just an ordinary day,
so I'll thank you
for the good things I often forget
I have.

Thank you for my eyes
with which I see my friends
and _____.

Thank you for my nose
with which I smell the fresh air
and _____.

Thank you for my ears
with which I hear laughter
and _____.

Thank you for my mouth
with which I taste good food
and _____.

Thank you for my hands
with which I clap and write and wave
and _____.

Thank you, Father,
for giving me life today.
Amen.

Prayer on a Day When I Feel Special

Father,
thank you
for letting me
be me.

You made me special.

No one else
is just like me.

No one ever will be
just like me.

I'm going to give you
a special gift today.

It's me.
Amen.

Prayer on a Bummer

Father,
some days are great,
some days are okay,
but today
was a bummer.

I hoped today
would be such fun,
but it sure wasn't.

I was expecting
the best day,
and it was
the worst.

But I give it to you, Father.

Maybe we need
some bad days
once in a while.
Then we can see how lucky
we are to have
so many
good days.

Thanks, God.

Prayer on a Snowy Day

Loving Father,
you gave us snow today.
It's fresh and new and beautiful.

We thank you for making
every snowflake different
from the others,
just as you make
each person different.

Every snowflake shows me
how wonderful you are.

Every person shows me
how loving you are.

Help me to be
the very best me
I can be.

Amen.

Prayer on an Empty Winter Day

Father,
this day seemed so long
and empty.

Same friends.
Same games.
Same schoolwork.

Old snow.
Melting ice rink.
A cold that hangs on and on.

I thought the day
looked empty,
but now
I'm remembering
a huge gift
you gave me—

I'm alive!

Thanks, God.

Prayer on a Spring Day

Father,
thank you for making
the whole world
come alive again
after the long winter.

Thank you for the joy
I felt today
when I saw flowers
about to open.

Each blue and white and yellow
and red flower
is a gift from you.

Thank you for showing
your love
through the beautiful things
you have made.

Amen.

Prayer on a Summer Day

God our Father,
this is
one of your perfect days.

It's warm and sunny
and the whole earth
smells good.

I can see and smell and touch
your love
all around me.

I see your love
in the woods and the garden.
I see your love
in the clear blue sky
and thick green grass.

I hear your love
in the songs of birds
and the sounds of kids laughing.

I feel your love
in the warm sand between my toes
and in the petals of flowers.

Thank you
for the beautiful world
you've given me.

Amen.

Prayer on an Empty Summer Day

Loving Father,
summer is getting boring.

We've run out
of things to do.

We're tired of each other.
But we're not ready
for school.

We're looking
for something different
or exciting
to happen.

This is our problem
for today.

Please give us
an idea
of what to do
with our time.

We ask this
in the name of Jesus.
Amen.

Prayer on a Fall Day

Father,
the world you made
seems to be winding down.

The sun sets earlier
every day;
the leaves are turning color
and falling.

Some days
are gray and shivery
and make the flowers
wilt and die.

Some days
are very, very warm,
so that I forget
about the gray, shivery days.

But whether it's brown and red and yellow
or gray and cold,
each day is a day you've given us.

Thank you, God.

Amen.

Prayer of Believing

God,
I believe in you.

I believe
everything you do
is good.

I believe
you have given me life.

I believe
you have shared
with us the greatest
of all gifts—
your Son, Jesus—
and through him,
your Holy Spirit.

I believe
my happiness
is in knowing and loving
you.

Thank you
for this gift
of believing.

Show me how
to make it grow.

Help me never to lose it.

I ask this in the name of Jesus.
Amen.

Prayer of Praise

God our Father,
we praise you!

We think you are wonderful
and kind
and good.

Every day
you show us
how great you are
and how much
you love us.

We want to shout,
"You are wonderful, God!"

Alleluia!

Prayer of Hoping

God,
you are always good,
and you always keep your promises.

I trust you
to forgive me
when I choose to do things
that hurt others.

Help me to be more like you
and to live with you
forever.

I ask this through Jesus,
my Lord and Savior. Amen.

Prayer of Loving

God,
you are wonderful,
and every part of me
loves you.

Because you have loved
me first
and taught me how
to love you,
I can reach out
to people around me
and share your love
with them.

I am sorry that sometimes
I have hurt
some of your people.

I forgive anyone
who has hurt me.

Be with us always, Father.
We need you.
Amen.

Prayer After Nine Rainy Days
(or Two or Three)

Loving Father,
we know
the rain you send
is a gift,
and we thank you.

We know our grass and plants
were very dry.
We know all your creatures
need water.

But all this rain
gets a little boring.

We're tired of being inside
or getting soaked
when we go outside.

Show us your sunshine
soon, Father.
And help us wait.
Amen.

Prayer After a Fight on the Playground

Father,
why are some kids
so mean
on the playground?

Why do they
punch and kick
or call me a dummy
when I make a mistake?

Why do they think
they have the right
to hurt other kids?

I don't understand it.

They really make me angry.
But I'm going to do
what your Son did.

I'm going to pray
for the kids who hurt me
and the kids who hurt
other kids.

You love us all
even when we're mean.

Tomorrow help us to have fun
instead of fights.

We ask this in the name of Jesus.
Amen.

A Family Forgiveness Prayer Service

Leader: Loving Father,
          our family gathers here
          together with you.

          Help us to listen carefully
          to our hearts tonight
          to see if we have shared
          our love and peace
          with each other,
          or if we have hurt
          each other.

          We know you love us very much.

          You are always ready
          to forgive us.
          Help us now
          to forgive each other.

Leader: First, let's listen to this story
          Jesus told about a forgiving father.

Child: There once was a man who had two sons.
          The younger son was unhappy. He
          wanted to leave home and have fun. He
          said to his father, "Give me my share of the
          family money." So the father gave each son
          his share of money.
                  The older son stayed at home to work
          with his father. The younger son left home
          and went far away. He ate fancy food,
          bought fine clothes, and gave big parties

for his friends. One day all his money was gone. So were all his friends. He was poor and sad and alone. He found a job feeding pigs. Sometimes he was so hungry that he felt like eating the pigs' food.

More than anything, he wanted to be home again in his father's house. So he left the pigs and started for home.

Meanwhile, the father waited at home, hoping that his younger son would return. Every day he watched the road for some sign of him. Then one day he saw someone in the distance. He knew it was his son, and he ran out to meet him.

The son said, "Father, I have sinned against God and you. I do not even deserve to be called your son. Just let me work as a servant in your house."

The father threw his arms around his son and kissed him. He was so happy that he shouted to the servants, "My son has come home! Get him new clothes and sandals. Prepare a celebration."

The older son came in from the fields. He was tired from his hard day's work. As he got closer to the house, he could hear music. "What is the reason for all the music and dancing?" he asked the servants.

"Your brother has come home. Your father is so happy he is giving a party," the servants answered.

The older son grew very angry. He would not go into the house and join the party.

Soon the father came outside to see his older son. The older son said, "Father, all these years I have been working by your side, but you have never given a party for me and my friends. This younger son of yours went away and wasted his money. Now, just because he has come home, you have a big celebration."

"My son," replied the father, "you are always with me. Everything I have is yours. But your brother went away and has come home again. We thought he was dead, and now he is with us. He was lost, and now he is found. We must all celebrate his return."

adapted from Luke 15:11-32

All: Thank you, God our Father, for always forgiving us when we are sorry.

Leader: Let's take a few minutes to talk together about the message of this story. (Discussion)

Leader: Let's be silent and think about a time when we turned away from God our Father and thought only of ourselves instead of helping others. (Pause)

All: We are sorry, Father.

Leader: Let's ask God's forgiveness for those times we have not obeyed his command to love all people.

All: We are sorry, Father.

Leader: For the times we have been mean or selfish to each other in our words,

All: We are sorry, Father.

Leader: For the times we have been mean or selfish to each other in our actions,

All: We are sorry, Father.

Leader: For the times we have refused to share our time or our things or our friendship,

All: We are sorry, Father.

Leader: For the times we have not welcomed others into our family,

All: We are sorry, Father.

Children: For the times we have not shown our love for our parents by obeying them,

All: We are sorry, Father.

Parents: For the times when we as parents have failed to listen to our children's needs,

All: We are sorry, Father.

Leader: For the times we have not done our share of the work,

All: We are sorry, Father.

Leader: For the times we have hurt each other by lying or telling only half the truth,

All: We are sorry, Father.

Leader: For the times we have not forgiven each other,

All: We are sorry, Father.

Leader: As a sign that we are willing to start over and be peaceful and loving again, let's share a sign of our peace with each other. (A hug, a kiss, a handshake)

Leader: Father, your Son Jesus said, "Peace I leave with you; my peace I give to you." Please give this family peace and love as we gather here for reconciliation.

All: Amen.

Leader: Let's end our prayer by joining hands and praying the prayer of forgiveness that Jesus taught us.

All: Our Father, who art in heaven . . . .

Our Family's Prayers for Every Day ❧❧❧❧

Prayers for Special Days

Prayer on a Graduation Day

God our Father,
we celebrate
a new beginning today
for our graduate, _____.

She (He) has worked hard
to use the gifts you gave her (him)
to learn and discover,
to understand and appreciate
this world you've given us.

Now,
as she (he) begins
a new time in her (his) life,
we ask that you help her (him)
to continue
to grow and to learn,
so that she (he) will become
the best she (he) can be.

Thank you, God.

Prayer on a Daughter's Birthday

Fill in the name and age of the person whose birthday you are celebrating.

Father,
we thank you
for _____
on her birthday.

We thank you
for giving her _____ years
with us.

We thank you
for the joy and love
she brings to our family.

We ask you
to keep her close to you
all the days of her life.

Please help her share
joy and love
with every person she meets.

We ask that you
help her learn
all she can about you.

Help her every day
to be loving,
so that someday
she'll be with you
in heaven.

Amen.

Family Record

~~~~~~~~~~~~

Birthday

_____
_____
_____
_____

Prayer on a Son's Birthday

Fill in the name and age of the person whose birthday you are celebrating.

Loving Father,
you've given us _____,
our son and brother.

Thank you
for the _____ years
he has given us smiles
and fun and happy thoughts.

Please help him
to be like you
in helping others.

Help him to know you better,
so that he can share
the love you've given him
all the days
of his life.

Keep him close to you, Lord,
so that someday
he'll be with you
forever in heaven.

Amen.

Name

_____

_____

_____

_____

Prayer on Mother's Day

God our Father,
today we thank you
for one
of your special gifts
to us—
our mother.

Thank you for the love
she shares with us
in so many ways.

We thank her
for the warmth she gives our home,
for the cuts and bruises she makes well,
for the ideas she gives us
when we don't have anything to do,
for all the times she talks and listens to us,
for the ways she makes peace
when we are mean to each other.

We thank her
for seeing good
in us
that we don't see
ourselves.
Help us to love her
as she loves us.

And keep her close to you
always.

We ask this in the name of Jesus.
Amen.

Prayer on Father's Day

Father,
we celebrate our dad today.
We celebrate
the special person he is.

We celebrate his love
for us
and our love
for him.

He is our friend,
our teller of good stories,
a listener to our problems,
and a helper in times of trouble.

Help us to show him
today and every day
how special he is
and how much
we love him.

Help us to be
as loving as he is.

Help him to continue
to be the best dad
he can be.

We ask this in the name of Jesus.
Amen.

Prayer on the Fourth of July

Father,
we celebrate
our freedom today.

We celebrate
living in this country
where we are free
to be the best
we can be.

Thank you
for all your blessings
on America —

*Mention special people, places, and events for which you
want to thank God especially this year.*

Please teach us
how to use
our freedom
to make all your people
happy.

Prayer About Going on Vacation

Father,
all good things
come from you,
and we thank you
that we are able
to take a vacation.

We thank you
for these days ahead
when we will enjoy new places
and new people
and new fun.

Please help us
to be kind
and thoughtful
of each other,
so that we can all relax
and get to know each other
better.

Keep us safe, Father,
and protect our home
and those we love.

Please take special care
of the people
who must work
while we celebrate
our vacation.

Prayer on a Wedding Day

Loving Father,
we celebrate today
the special love
of these two special persons,
_____ and _____.

We ask you to bless them
and to surround their love
with your own love and care.

Father,
we ask you
to keep them close to you
so that they may learn
to know and love each other
unselfishly.

May this man and woman
help each other
to become
all that each of them
can be.

In all they do,
show them the path
to peace, love, and joy
so that one day
they will share
happiness forever with you.

Amen.

Prayer Before the First Day of School

Loving Father,
we aren't sure
we feel like celebrating today,
because tomorrow
is the first day of school.

Some kids like school;
some kids don't.
Some days *we* like school;
some days *we* don't.

There's a strange feeling
inside
because we don't know
what's coming.

We give you this feeling, Father,
and this year of school.

Please be with us
so we'll look for what's good
in each day
and then do our very best.

Prayer to Celebrate Baptism

Use on the day of a Baptism, on the anniversary of a Baptism, or on any day as a reminder of God's special gifts.

Father,
we celebrate
your life in us
today.

Thank you
for calling us
to be Christians
and members
of your family.

Help us
to believe in you
and to follow you
always.

Family Record

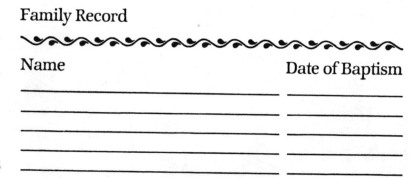

Name   Date of Baptism

Prayer to Celebrate First Communion

Use on a First Communion Day or
anniversary of a First Communion.

Father,
I am celebrating your love
again today.

I am celebrating
my First Communion.

I believe
Jesus is present to us
in a special way
in the bread and wine.

I believe
you share your life with us
in Jesus' Body and Blood.

Thank you
for so much love.

Help us to love as you do.

I ask this in Jesus' name.
Amen.

Family Record

Name	Date of First Communion

Prayer to Celebrate Confirmation

*Use on a Confirmation Day or
anniversary of a Confirmation.*

God our Father,
thank you
for the special gift
of your Holy Spirit.

Help me to share
this same Spirit
with every person I meet.

I need your Holy Spirit
to teach me the right things
to choose
so that I can follow you
each day.

I need your Spirit
to help me be kind
even when others
are not kind to me.

I need your Spirit
to help me be gentle
even when others
are not gentle with me.

I need your Spirit
to help me listen
even when others
don't listen to me.

Make your gifts new again
in me, Father.
Amen.

Prayer on My Parents' Wedding Anniversary

Father,
we are celebrating
two special people today.

_____ years ago
Mom and Dad
promised to love each other
always.

Today
we celebrate
their love.

We ask you
to help their love grow
stronger
and deeper
forever.

We ask this in the name of Jesus.
Amen.

Prayer on the Feast of Easter

God our loving Father,
we are your people
and everything in us
shouts out for joy
on this feast of the Resurrection.

What great love and power
you have shown!
You have raised your Son Jesus
from death!

You have given him a new life
stronger than death.
You have made him Lord
over all the earth.

In the name of all your creatures
we thank you for your great love.
We praise you
and we wait with hope
for the day
of our own resurrection.

Show us that we can celebrate
the new life of Easter
today and every day
through the truth,
the hope,
and the love
we give each other
in the name of our risen Lord.
Amen.

Prayer on Thanksgiving Day

God our Father,
we gather together
with those we love
on this Thanksgiving Day
to celebrate
your many gifts to us.

You are truly
a loving Father
who cares for all our needs.

We also remember
that many
of your children
cannot celebrate today
because
they are hungry
or homeless
or have no one
to love them.

Please show us
how we can share
our gifts
with them.
Amen.

Prayer During the First Week of Advent
Use with the Advent wreath or other Advent custom.

Father,
it's that wonderful time
of the year again.

We're going to celebrate
your Son's birthday soon.

We will be preparing our home,
our gifts,
our food.

Help us to remember
to prepare our hearts.

Help us in all our busyness
to remember
it's your Son
we're getting ready for.

Help us
help a friend,
keep a promise,
or visit someone lonely.

Come, Lord Jesus!
We need you.

Prayer During the Second Week of Advent

Mary,
for you this time
before Jesus' birthday
was a quiet time,
a growing time.

Now we are all
waiting
for your Son Jesus.

Mary, mother of Jesus
and our mother,
show us
how to be ready
for your Son.

Come, Jesus!
The whole world
is waiting
for you.

Prayer During the Third Week of Advent

Lord,
we're waiting
and waiting
and waiting.

Christmas
still seems so far away.

Who are we, Lord
that you,
our king,
will come again and again
to give us your love?

Thank you
for wanting to be
with us
always.

Help us to make room
inside
for all your love.

Please help us right now
to make
a silent space
inside
just for you.

Let us all stop now for a moment of silence.

Come, Lord Jesus!

Prayer During the Fourth Week of Advent

We are eager
for your birthday,
Lord Jesus.

We love the tinsel
on the tree
and the decorations
all around.

We love the making
and the wrapping,
and we love
the secrets
under beds.

But most of all
we love you, Lord.

We love you
for loving us
so much
that you wanted to be
a human being
just like us.

Thank you
for becoming a child
and showing us
how to grow.

Come, Lord Jesus!
We are waiting for you.

Prayer on the Feast of Christmas

God our Father,
it's Christmas at last.
Thank you
for this big celebration.

We are happy
because you have given us
your greatest gift of love,
Jesus your Son.

We welcome Jesus
and we thank you
for all the love
and hope and peace
he brings us.

Help us to be like Jesus
and bring love and hope and peace
to each other.

Let the love
in our family
reach out
to everyone we meet
today and tomorrow
and every day.

Prayer on the Sunday After Christmas

Lord,
it's quiet now.

The glitter and the noise,
the excitement and the feasting
are winding down.

In this rest and peace
after the celebration of Christmas,
let us quietly think
of you
and your love
and your peace.

Thank you for coming to us.

Please stay with us always.

Our Family's Prayers for Special Days

Prayers for Special People

Prayer for Our Leaders

God our Father,
today we pray
for people
who have the big job
of being in charge
of other people—
our leaders.

Since your ways
are all good
and your ideas
are all wise,
please share
your goodness and wisdom
with these leaders.

Show them clearly
your love and your law
so that they will
lead us
to you.
Amen.

Prayer for My Family

Loving Father,
today we celebrate
this group of special people,
our family.

It isn't anyone's birthday;
we just want to say
thank you
for making us a family.

We're glad
we have each other.

Thank you for the times
you have helped us
to understand
and love
and forgive
each other.

Help us to know how much
we need each other.

Help us to remember how much
we need you.

Help us to grow together
so that someday
we'll be together again
with you
in heaven.
Amen.

Prayer About a New Baby

Loving Father,
you share life
with us
in so many ways.

Now you have given our family
a new little child,
and we thank you.

We are filled
with wonder
at her (his) smallness.
We praise you
for such perfection.

Please help us
to show our new baby
how to grow up
full of love.

Please help us
to show her (him)
the joy
of being Christian.

Prayer During a Family Upset

Father,
this is a hard time for us.

We have a problem,
and we need your help
to solve it.

Some days it's easy
to share our family love.

But some days,
like today,
we just seem to bother
each other.

Please help us now
to put our problem
into words
and solve it.

Thank you for loving us, Father.
Amen.

Prayer for a Friend

Fill in the name of your friend.

God our Father,
thank you for my friend _____.
He (She) cares for me
and did something nice
for me today.

I am thinking
what a good friend
you are
and how you have
always loved me
and always will.

Father, help me
to be a good friend, too—
always loving,
always caring.

In Jesus' name.
Amen.

Prayer for a Friend With a Problem
Fill in the name of your friend.

Jesus,
you said whoever needs you
should come and talk
to you.

My friend _____
has a problem
and needs you;
only I'm not sure
he's (she's) going to remember
to talk to you about it.

So I'm here to tell you.

Please send your Holy Spirit
to give him (her) an idea
for solving this problem.

Thank you for hearing me, Lord.

Prayer for a Sad Friend

Fill in the name of your friend.

Loving Father,
my friend _____
is sad today.

Please help me
to share your love
with him (her)
and make
the sadness easier.

Prayer for a Sick Person in the Family
Fill in the name of the sick person.

Father,
we love you.
We trust you.
We don't want _____
to be sick.

We ask you
to help _____ get well
and to be patient
while she (he) is sick.

We know you'll help her (him), Father.

And please help all sick people,
especially those
who have no one
to pray for them
or take care of them.

Thank you for hearing our prayer.
In the name of Jesus. Amen.

Prayer About the Older Folks

Father,
we're praying today
for some friends of yours
who have known you
for many, many years—
the older people.

We pray for grandmas and grandpas
and for all who have lived
on your earth for a long time.

We pray that the rest of us
will love them and care for them.

We pray especially
for older people who are sick
or lonely
or worried
or afraid.

Be gentle with them, Father,
and help them to be patient
and young
in their hearts.

Amen.

69

Prayer About a Death in the Family
Fill in the name of the person who has died.

Loving Father,
our hearts are sad
because _____ has died.

You have called her (his) name
and we know she (he) went
with great joy
to be with you
forever in heaven.

We ask that _____
watch over us
just as she (he) did
on this earth.

Thank you
for the love and happiness
she (he) shared
with each of us.

Please give us
courage
to live now as she (he) did—
with great love and happiness.

And let us all be together
again someday, Father.
Amen.

Prayer About the Death of a Pet

Fill in the name of your pet.

Loving Father,
you have given us
everything good—
the nights and days,
the sun and moon,
the lakes and rivers,
the trees and every kind
of flower.
You have given us every creature,
and you gave us _____, our pet.

But now_____ has died
and gone back to the earth.

_____ gave us great fun
and was such a good friend.
_____ even helped us
to share our love.

We miss _____ very much.

We ask you to fill up
the empty space
in our hearts.

We ask you to let
something beautiful grow
from the earth where _____ rests.

Thank you, Father,
for all your gifts.

Fido

Prayer for Unhappy and Forgotten People

Loving Father,
some of your people
are hurting.

They have problems
that are very hard
to solve.

Many are sad;
many are poor;
many are rich,
but sad and poor
inside.

And many don't have a single friend.

Please help
all these people, Father,
and show us
how we can share
your love
with them.

Prayer for Someone I Could Have Helped and Didn't

Father,
I had a chance
to share my love today,
but I didn't.

Someone needed me,
but I passed right by.
I pretended not to see
because I was enjoying
what I was doing
and didn't want to stop.

I'm sorry
I didn't help.
Please give him (her)
the love I didn't share.

Our Family's Prayers for Special People

Prayers for When I'm by Myself

Prayer at a Time of Disappointment

God,
I've prayed so long
and hoped so hard,
but things don't seem
to get better.

I love you
and I want to trust you.

You know what's best for me.

I don't understand right now,
but I know
you'll take care of things.

You'll answer my prayer
in your own way.

Thank you, God.

Prayer When I'm Sick

Lord Jesus,
I don't like being sick.
I'm stuck here in bed
and I'm tired of reading
and watching TV.

Help me think of you
and pretend that I'm one
of the children
who climbed up on your lap
and sat very close to you.

Maybe you would look me
right in the eye and say,
"You are my friend
and my brother (sister).
You are a very special person,
and there is no one else
just like you.
I love you very much."

And you'd put your hands
on my head and say,
"I ask my Father
to bless you and your family
and to help you
to love him
as I do."

Jesus,
help me to think some more
about you.

Let me listen
to what you are saying
to me.

79

Prayer During the Chicken Pox

Father,
I didn't know
I could itch so much
and not go crazy.

I don't know why
you allow
such a misery
as chicken pox,
but you must have a reason.

I know there will be an end
to the itch
and the ugliness,
and I ask you to help me
to be patient
until it's gone.

I ask you to help
all children
who are much sicker
than I am,
especially those
who won't ever get well.

Prayer on an Angry Day

Father,
this morning I woke up
unhappy,
and that's how my day was.

It was one of those days
when I was on the wrong side
of everything.

I felt selfish and mean,
and I hurt some feelings.

I'm still unhappy,
but now I'm sorry.

Help me to love those
I hurt.

Help them to forgive me.

Amen.

Prayer for Someone Who Hurt My Feelings

God our Father,
I'm sad to say
somebody's feelings were hurt
today,
and this time they were mine.

I was trying so hard,
but someone laughed at me.
I felt a lump in my throat
and I tried not to cry.

Please help me to forgive her (him)
for hurting my feelings.

Please give her (him)
more of your love,
so she (he) will care more
about other people's feelings.

I ask this in the name of Jesus.
Amen.

Prayer About Someone Who Bothers Me

Lord Jesus,
you said I should love
all people,
even my enemies.

That's very hard to do,
but I guess
you know all about that.

You know that a certain person
seems to enjoy
hurting my feelings
and calling me names
and making fun
of anything I do well.

I try to treat him (her)
the same way
I'd like him (her)
to treat me.
But he (she) doesn't even notice.

How can he (she) enjoy
being mean?

Maybe he's (she's) unhappy
inside himself (herself)
so he (she) doesn't know
he (she) has any love
to share.

Please teach him (her)
how to love
and help me
to do the same.

Thanks, God.

Prayer About Failure

Loving Father,
I've made a mess of things.

I set out
to do my best
but I didn't succeed.

I feel empty and lonely inside.

But something tells me
that my family
and my friends
and you still love me.

I guess the one
I failed the most
is me.

Help me
to forgive myself, Father.

Prayer About Brothers and Sisters

God my Father,
I know you made
all creatures
with great love
and you want us
to love them
as you do.

But some days
it's hard for me to love
all your creatures.

Today was a day
when I didn't want
to love my brother (sister).

It's hard to think of love
when he (she) is teasing
or bossy.

We couldn't agree
on anything,
and everything we tried
ended in an argument.

Father,
you know we care
about each other.

Please help us
to solve our problems
peacefully
and with love.

Thanks, God.

Prayer When I'm Lonely

Jesus,
you are a friend
to all your people.
You told us
to come to you
at any time.

Right now
I need you
very much.

I feel very much alone
and in need of a friend.

I think
this empty and sad feeling
is one of the worst
there is,
and I'm praying for me
and for everyone
who is lonely at this moment.

You felt lonely sometimes.
What did you do
about it?
Please come
and help me fill
the emptiness.

Prayer About Fear

God,
you are my Father
and I know
you love me very much.
I know you care
about everything
I do.

When I remember
your love,
I am not afraid
of anything.

But when I forget
how you love me,
many things
can make me afraid.

Let me put my hand
in yours, Father.

Keep me close to you
so that fear
will go away
and I will be brave.

Amen.

Prayer When I Need the Holy Spirit

God our Father,
thank you
for sharing your Holy Spirit
with me.

You give me your Spirit
to teach me
how to be truthful
and loving
and ready to do
what pleases you.

Right now
I have a big decision
to make.

Help me
to listen to your Spirit
so that I will make
choices that honor you
and will be the best person
I can be.

Prayer in the Night
Make a copy of this prayer to keep near your bed.

Our Father,
I'm scared.

It's late at night
and everyone is sleeping
but me.

It's very dark
and I'm very lonely.

Please help me
not to be afraid.

Please help me
understand that
you are here
with me
now.

I'm going to say "Our Father"
over and over
until I fall asleep again.

Did you wake me up
so I could talk to you?